3 9082 14519 5098

D1716517

AUBURN HILLS PUBLIC LIBRARY 50
3400 EAST SEYBURN DRIVE
AUBURN HILLS, MI 48326
(248) 370-9466

COUNTRY 🌐 PROFILES

SOUTH KOREA

BY ALICIA Z. KLEPEIS

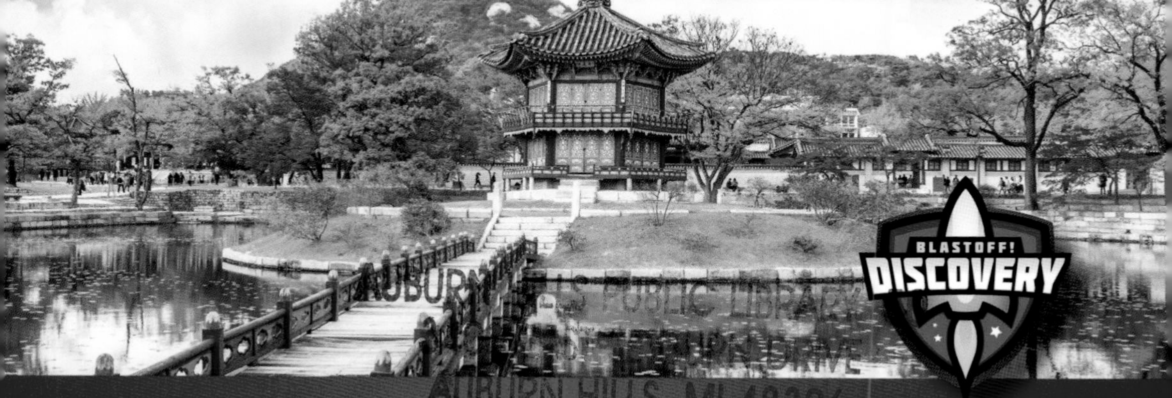

BLASTOFF!
DISCOVERY

BELLWETHER MEDIA • MINNEAPOLIS, MN

Blastoff! Discovery launches a new mission: reading to learn. Filled with facts and features, each book offers you an exciting new world to explore!

This edition first published in 2020 by Bellwether Media, Inc.

No part of this publication may be reproduced in whole or in part without written permission of the publisher.
For information regarding permission, write to Bellwether Media, Inc., Attention: Permissions Department,
6012 Blue Circle Drive, Minnetonka, MN 55343.

Library of Congress Cataloging-in-Publication Data

Names: Klepeis, Alicia, 1971- author.
Title: South Korea / by Alicia Z. Klepeis.
Description: Minneapolis, MN : Bellwether Media, Inc., 2020. |
   Series: Blastoff! Discovery : country profiles | Includes
   bibliographical references and index. | Audience: Ages: 7-13 |
   Audience: Grades: 4-6 | Summary: "Engaging images accompany
   information about South Korea. The combination of high-interest
   subject matter and narrative text is intended for students in grades
   3 through 8"– Provided by publisher.
Identifiers: LCCN 2019034845 (print) | LCCN 2019034846 (ebook)
   | ISBN 9781644871720 (library binding) | ISBN
   9781618918482 (ebook)
Subjects: LCSH: Korea (South)–Juvenile literature. | Korea (South)–
   Social life and customs–Juvenile literature.
Classification: LCC DS907.4 .K58 2020 (print) | LCC DS907.4
   (ebook) | DDC 951.95–dc23
LC record available at https://lccn.loc.gov/2019034845
LC ebook record available at https://lccn.loc.gov/2019034846

Text copyright © 2020 by Bellwether Media, Inc. BLASTOFF!
DISCOVERY and associated logos are trademarks
and/or registered trademarks of Bellwether Media, Inc.

Editor: Rebecca Sabelko   Designer: Brittany McIntosh

Printed in the United States of America, North Mankato, MN.

TABLE OF CONTENTS

BEAUTIFUL BUSAN

It is a warm summer morning when a group of **tourists** arrives in Busan. They begin their day on the waterfront of this port city. Vendors at the Jagalchi Fish Market call out, offering octopus and squid. The air smells of salt.

BUSAN TOWER

OTHER TOP SITES

GYEONGBOKGUNG PALACE

HALLASAN

LOTTE WORLD

NAKSANSA TEMPLE

After a short train ride and walk, the group arrives at Yongdusan Park. They picnic near a clock made of flowers. Next, they ride the elevator to the top of Busan Tower. The view of the entire city is incredible! At night, they ride the Songdo Marine Cable Car. City lights twinkle as they glide over the sea. Welcome to South Korea!

5

LOCATION

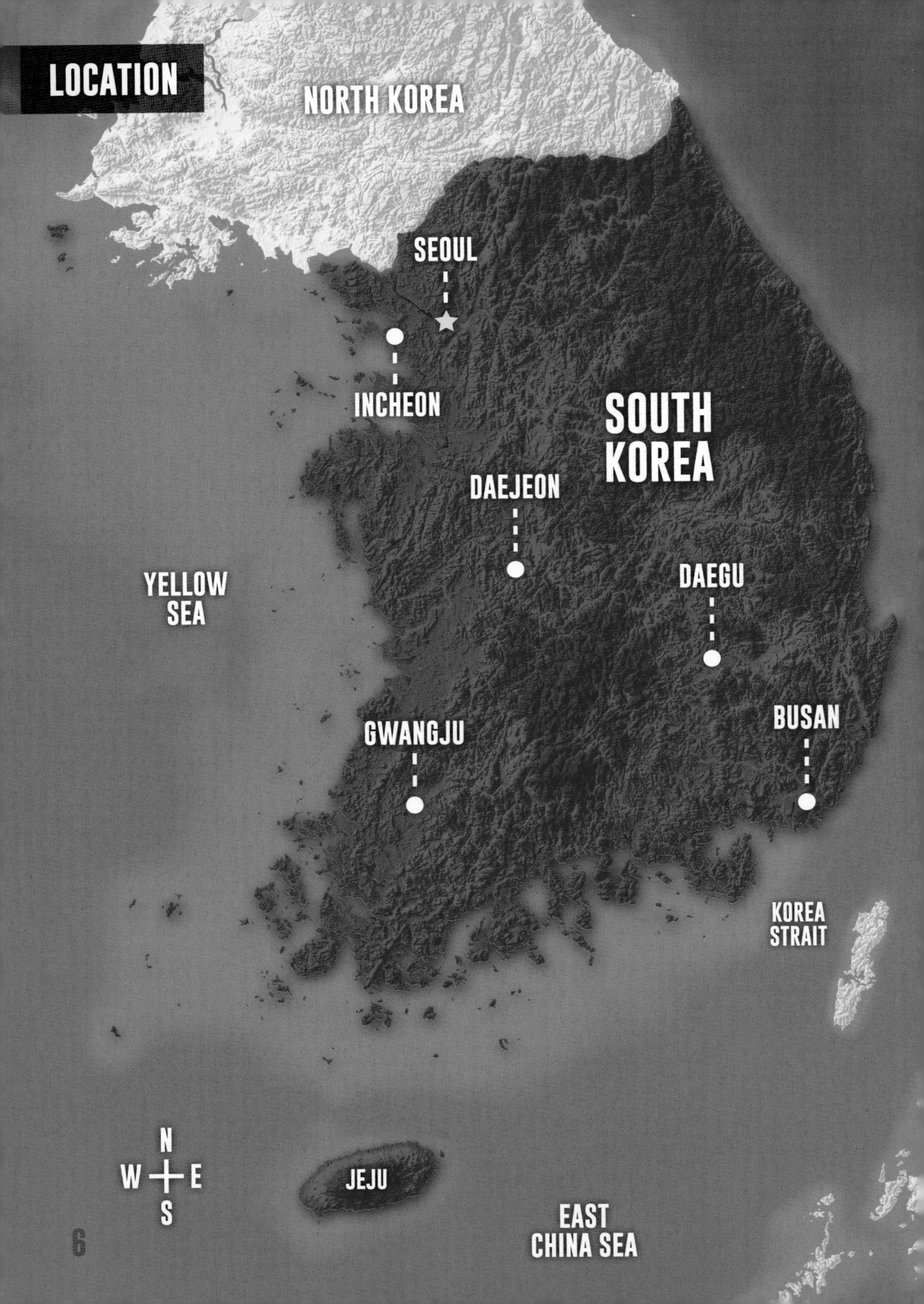
NORTH KOREA
SEOUL
INCHEON
SOUTH KOREA
DAEJEON
YELLOW SEA
DAEGU
BUSAN
GWANGJU
KOREA STRAIT
N
W
E
S
JEJU
EAST CHINA SEA

South Korea is located on the Korean **Peninsula** in East Asia. It covers 38,502 square miles (99,720 square kilometers). Seoul, the capital, is in the country's northwest. The nation's second-largest city, Busan, lies on the southeast coast.

North Korea, the only country that directly borders South Korea, is its northern neighbor. Waves from the Sea of Japan crash on South Korea's eastern shores. To the southeast, the Korea **Strait** separates South Korea from Japan. The East China Sea forms the country's southern coastline. Waves of the Yellow Sea wash onto the west coast.

ISLAND OF WONDERS

Jeju Island is home to the country's highest mountain, a variety of wildlife, and beautiful beaches. It is one of the New Seven Wonders of Nature!

SEA OF JAPAN

JAPAN

LANDSCAPE AND CLIMATE

Overall, South Korea is a nation with rugged **terrain**. The Sobaek Mountains wind across the Korean Peninsula. Along the country's east coast run the Taebaek Mountains. The Naktong and Han Rivers both begin in this range. Along South Korea's west and south coasts are mudflats. There are also narrow **plains** along the coastline.

= TAEBAEK MOUNTAINS   = SOBAEK MOUNTAINS

HAN RIVER

NAKTONG RIVER

NAKTONG RIVER

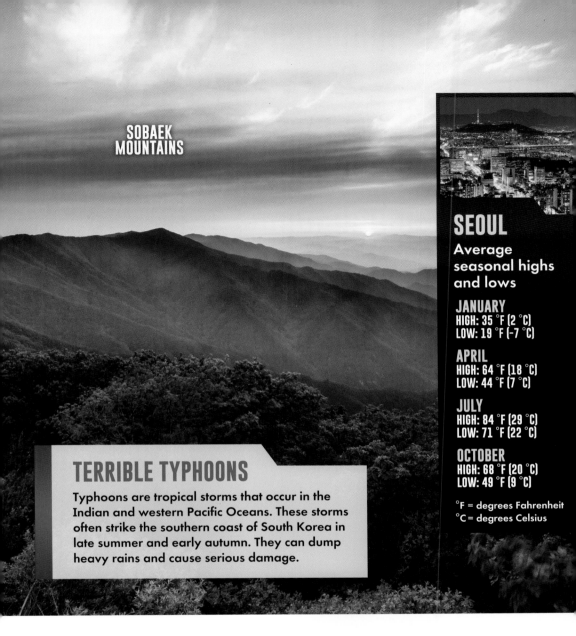

SOBAEK
MOUNTAINS

SEOUL
Average seasonal highs and lows

JANUARY
HIGH: 35 °F (2 °C)
LOW: 19 °F (-7 °C)

APRIL
HIGH: 64 °F (18 °C)
LOW: 44 °F (7 °C)

JULY
HIGH: 84 °F (29 °C)
LOW: 71 °F (22 °C)

OCTOBER
HIGH: 68 °F (20 °C)
LOW: 49 °F (9 °C)

°F = degrees Fahrenheit
°C = degrees Celsius

TERRIBLE TYPHOONS

Typhoons are tropical storms that occur in the Indian and western Pacific Oceans. These storms often strike the southern coast of South Korea in late summer and early autumn. They can dump heavy rains and cause serious damage.

South Korea has a **continental** climate. Its winters are cold and relatively dry. Summers are hot and humid. Most of the nation's rain falls during the summer **monsoons** lasting from June to August.

There is not as much wildlife present in South Korea today as there was in the past. Animals such as lynx and bears have largely disappeared. Many reptile and fish species are also threatened. This is due to pollution and heavy use of the land for farming and other activities.

The DMZ, or Demilitarized Zone, is the area between South and North Korea. It has become a **refuge** for wildlife. **Migratory** red-crowned cranes soar overhead as musk deer roam in search of plants to eat. Asiatic black bears munch on fruits and insects. Spotted seals swim in the waters of the DMZ.

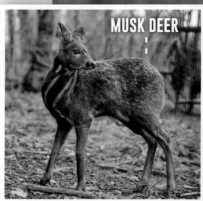
MUSK DEER

SPOTTED SEAL

BLUE ROCK-THRUSH

ASIATIC BLACK BEAR

DADOHAEHAESANG NATIONAL PARK

Dadohaehaesang is South Korea's biggest national park. More than 140 kinds of birds, including the blue rock-thrush, live here.

RED-CROWNED
CRANE

RED-CROWNED CRANE

Life Span: 30 years
Red List Status: endangered

red-crowned crane range =

LEAST CONCERN	NEAR THREATENED	VULNERABLE	ENDANGERED	CRITICALLY ENDANGERED	EXTINCT IN THE WILD	EXTINCT

More than 51 million people live in South Korea. Almost all South Koreans belong to the Korean **ethnic** group. A small number of Chinese and Southeast Asian people live in the country, too.

South Korea has no official religion. About one out of four South Koreans are Christian. Buddhism is the second-most practiced religion. Many people also follow some practices and **traditions** of **Confucianism**. More than half of all South Koreans do not practice any religion. Korean is the country's official language. It is written in a script called *Hangul*. South Korean students also learn English beginning in elementary school.

FAMOUS FACE

Name: Shin-Soo Choo
Birthday: July 13, 1982
Hometown: Busan, South Korea
Famous for: A Major League Baseball outfielder who was selected to play in the 2018 MLB All-Star Game

SPEAK KOREAN

Korean uses script instead of letters. However, Korean words can be written with the English alphabet so you can read them.

ENGLISH	KOREAN	HOW TO SAY IT
hello	annyeong haseyo	ahn-yung hah-say-YO
goodbye	annyeonghi gaseyo	ahn-yung-hee kah-say-YO
please	juseyo	choo-say-OH
thank you	gamsahamnida	KAHM-sahm-neeh-DAH
yes	ye	yeh
no	aniyo	ahn-ni-YO

BUSAN

COMMUNITIES

More than four out of five South Koreans live in **urban** areas. Seoul is the country's largest city, with nearly 10 million people. Most people in South Korea live in tall apartment buildings that may be 20 or even 30 stories high. It is more common to have stand-alone homes in **rural** areas. People in Korean cities often travel by bus, train, or car. People in rural areas often travel in their own cars.

SEOUL

TERRIFIC TRAINS

South Korea has an amazing high-speed rail network. KTX trains can reach 190 miles (305 kilometers) per hour! A trip from Busan to Seoul takes a little over two hours. That is about half the time an ordinary train takes!

About 95 out of every 100 South Koreans own smartphones. This is more than any other country. The nation's internet networks are among the world's fastest!

DOLJANCHI PARTIES

A Doljanchi party celebrates the first birthday of a Korean baby. Some wealthy parents throw big, fancy parties for their sons and daughters. Other parents choose to donate money to charity.

The traditional way South Koreans greet each other is with a short bow. Children, for example, will bow when greeting grown-ups. Men also shake hands when meeting. Before entering someone's house, people take off their shoes. Guests often sit on floor cushions.

South Koreans typically dress like people in the United States or Europe. On special occasions, they may wear *hanbok*. These traditional outfits are often colorful. Women wear a short jacket and a long, flowy skirt with layers of undergarments beneath. Men wear a long jacket and wide-legged pants.

HANBOK

Children in South Korea start primary school at age 6. Students attend six years of primary school, followed by three years of middle school. Almost all South Korean students go on to either **vocational** or academic high schools. Students must take difficult exams to get into colleges and universities.

About 7 out of 10 South Koreans have **service jobs**. Some work in offices, schools, or shopping malls. Others have jobs in the tourism industry. Workers **manufacture** products including computers, ships, and cars. Farmers grow rice, soybeans, and fruits and vegetables. They also make dairy products and raise livestock such as pigs.

CASHIERS

FANTASTIC FISHERIES

Both deep-sea and coastal fishing are important to South Korea. Squid, crab, tuna, and anchovies are some commonly fished species. People also raise fish to sell.

19

TAE KWON DO

Soccer, volleyball, and baseball are some of the most popular sports in South Korea. People also enjoy playing table tennis, badminton, and tennis. A traditional form of wrestling called *ssirŭm* is often practiced, as is the martial art *tae kwon do*. South Koreans hike, ski, and camp in the country's 22 national parks.

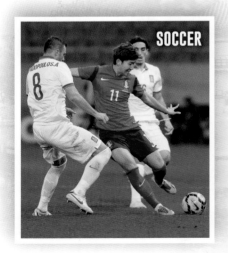

SOCCER

Video games are popular with young South Koreans. Young men also play billiards. Coworkers or friends may enjoy karaoke in their free time. Family and friends often play a card game called Go Stop. Players aim to collect sets of matching cards.

VIDEO GAME TOURNAMENT

MAKE A SOGO DRUM

Sogo drums are double-headed folk drums.

What You Need:
- 2 heavyweight paper plates
- a stapler
- glue
- 2 straight sticks
- colored markers

Instructions:
1. Put the two plates together with their bottoms facing outward. Staple the plates together. You will want to staple all the way around the edge of the plates, about every 0.5 inch (1 centimeter).

2. Take one of the sticks and push it between two staples somewhere along the edges of your drum. Glue the stick to keep it in place.

3. Once the glue is dry, use your markers to decorate your drum. Some Korean sogo drums have yin-yang symbols on them. But you can create your own design.

4. Use the remaining stick to beat your new drum!

INCREDIBLE ICE POPS

In South Korea, ice pops come in many flavors including melon, mango, banana, and plain milk. Jaws is a South Korean ice pop in the shape of a shark. It is grayish-purple on the outside and pink on the inside!

People in South Korea cook with a variety of spices. Chili gives heat to many popular dishes such as *buldak*, or fire chicken. A spicy red paste called *ssamjang* also adds heat and flavor to dishes including barbequed beef called *bulgogi*.

Almost every South Korean meal includes rice and *kimchi*, or **fermented** vegetables. A commonly eaten dish is *bibimbap*. It is made with seasoned vegetables and rice and usually topped with an egg.

BULGOGI

KIMCHI

People also eat a lot of seafood, such as octopus and clams. South Koreans enjoy fruits such as clementines and grapes for dessert.

KOREAN SESAME SEED COOKIES

Have an adult help you make this recipe.

Ingredients:
1 cup butter
3/4 cup white sugar
3/4 cup brown sugar
2 eggs
1 teaspoon baking soda
1 teaspoon hot water
1 1/2 teaspoons vanilla extract
3 cups flour
3/4 cup sesame seeds

Steps:
1. Preheat the oven to 325 degrees Fahrenheit (163 degrees Celsius). Toast the sesame seeds in a small pan until lightly golden.

2. In a bowl, combine the butter and sugars. Add the eggs and beat well.

3. Add hot water, baking soda, and vanilla extract to the sugar mixture. Then stir in the flour and sesame seeds. Cover the bowl and chill for about an hour.

4. Bake teaspoon-sized balls on a baking sheet for 10 to 12 minutes. Let them cool and enjoy!

CELEBRATIONS

People in South Korea celebrate *Seollal* in late January or early February. This three-day holiday celebrates the **lunar** New Year. South Koreans visit extended family and exchange gifts. People eat special foods such as *tteokguk*, or rice cake soup. They also honor their **ancestors** by performing certain ceremonies.

SEOLLAL

LIBERATION DAY

August 15 is Liberation Day. This holiday marks when Korea was freed from Japanese rule after World War II ended. People display flags in front of their homes and have the day off from work.

Many celebrations in South Korea are religious holidays. In April or May, Buddhists celebrate the birth of Buddha. They worship and decorate their temples with pink lanterns shaped like lotus flowers. Christian Koreans celebrate Easter and Christmas, among other holidays. South Koreans celebrate their country and **culture** throughout the year!

TIMELINE

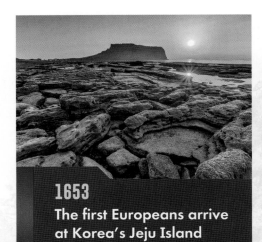

1948
The Republic of Korea is established

1653
The first Europeans arrive at Korea's Jeju Island

1392
The Choson dynasty begins rule over Korea

1910
Japan gains control of Korea

668-935
The Unified Silla Kingdom rules over the entire Korean Peninsula

1945
American troops occupy the southern area of the Korean Peninsula after WWII

1963
Two years after gaining power, Park Chung-hee brings freedom and industrialization to the nation

1987
South Korea has its first free presidential election

1950
South Korea demands independence from the Republic of Korea, sparking the Korean War

2018
South Korea hosts the Winter Olympics in Pyongchang

Official Name: Republic of Korea

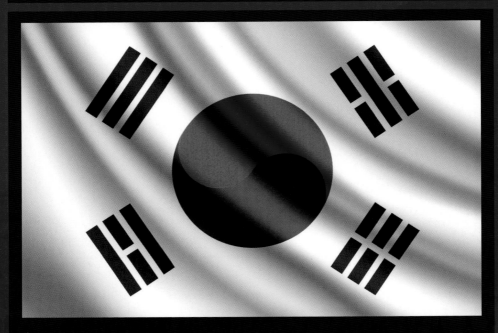

Flag of South Korea: South Korea's flag has a white background. In Korean culture, white represents purity and peace. In the center of the flag is a red and blue yin-yang symbol. The red stands for positive forces while the blue represents negative forces. In each corner of the flag is a black trigram, or *kwae*. Each one stands for one of the four universal elements: water, wind, earth, and fire. Together, these kwae express harmony.

Area: 38,502 square miles
(99,720 square kilometers)

Capital City: Seoul

Important Cities: Busan, Incheon, Daegu, Daejeon, Gwangju

Population:
51,418,097 (July 2018)

COUNTRYSIDE
18.5%

WHERE
PEOPLE LIVE

CITY
81.5%

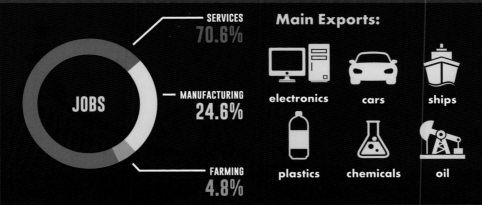

SERVICES
70.6%

JOBS

MANUFACTURING
24.6%

FARMING
4.8%

Main Exports:

electronics   cars   ships

plastics   chemicals   oil

National Holiday:
Liberation Day (August 15)

Main Languages:
Korean and English

Form of Government:
presidential republic

Title for Country Leaders:
president (head of state),
prime minister (head of government)

NONE
56.9%

RELIGION

BUDDHIST
15.5%

CATHOLIC
7.9%

PROTESTANT
19.7%

Unit of Money:
South Korean won

GLOSSARY

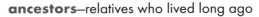

ancestors—relatives who lived long ago

Confucianism—a system of teachings developed by the Chinese philosopher Confucius

continental—relating to a relatively dry climate with very cold winters and very hot summers

culture—the beliefs, arts, and ways of life in a place or society

ethnic—related to a group of people who share customs and an identity

fermented—related to a substance that has gone through a chemical breakdown; vegetables can be fermented to create a certain flavor.

lunar—relating to the moon

manufacture—to make products, often with machines

migratory—referring to animals that travel from one place to another, often with the seasons

monsoons—winds that shift direction each season; monsoons bring heavy rain.

peninsula—a section of land that extends out from a larger piece of land and is almost completely surrounded by water

plains—large areas of flat land

refuge—a place that provides protection or shelter

rural—related to the countryside

service jobs—jobs that perform tasks for people or businesses

strait—a narrow channel connecting two bodies of water

terrain—the surface features of an area of land

tourists—people who travel to visit another place

traditions—customs, ideas, or beliefs handed down from one generation to the next

urban—related to cities and city life

vocational—referring to education or training directed at a particular job and its skills

TO LEARN MORE

AT THE LIBRARY

Henzel, Cynthia Kennedy. *Moon Jae-In: President of South Korea*. Lake Elmo, Minn.: Focus Readers, 2019.

Perkins, Chloe. *South Korea*. New York, N.Y.: Simon Spotlight, 2017.

Sullivan, Laura L. *South Korea*. New York, N.Y.: Cavendish Square Publishing, 2019.

ON THE WEB

Factsurfer.com gives you a safe, fun way to find more information.

1. Go to www.factsurfer.com.

2. Enter "South Korea" into the search box and click 🔍.

3. Select your book cover to see a list of related web sites.

INDEX

The images in this book are reproduced through the courtesy of: CJ Nattanai, front cover; catmanc, pp. 4-5; Teerachat paibung, p. 5 (Gyeongbokgung Palace); ju999, p. 5 (Hallasan); Guitar photographer, p. 5 (Lotte World); Aleksandr Sadkov, p. 5 (Nakansa Temple); unununius photo, p. 8; ESB Professional, p. 9 (top); Sangwon Nam, p. 9 (bottom); Aumsama, p. 10 (asiatic black bear); Suvorov_Alex, p. 10 (musk deer); Valerijs Novickis, p. 10 (spotted seal); Michele Aldeghi, p. 10 (blue rock-thrush); SanderMeertinsPhotography, pp. 10-11; Steven May / Alamy Stock Photo, p. 12; Keeton Gale, p. 12 (top); Panwasin seemala, p. 12 (bottom); july7th, pp. 14, 19, (bottom); NavyBank, p. 15; TongRo Image / Alamy Stock Photo, p. 16; Artaporn Puthikampol, p. 17; Christian Science Monitor / Contributor, p. 18; Sorbis, p. 19 (top); Yeongsik Im, p. 20 (top); Kotas Koutsaftikis, p. 20 (bottom); adamziaja.com, p. 21 (top); paula sierra, p. 21 (bottom); fotoVoyager, p. 22; Brent Hofacker, p. 23 (top); TMON, p. 23 (middle); Daria Minaeva, p. 23 (bottom); Chung Sung-Jun / Staff, p. 24; Pool / Pool, p. 25; Noppasin Wongchum, p. 26; Beautiful Korea, p. 27 (top); Sagase48, p. 27 (bottom); Ivan Vdovin / Alamy Stock Photo, p. 29 (bill); Yaroslaff, p. 29 (coin).